☞ **W9-BCI-654**

Sports IN ACTION

In-line Skating in Action

John Crossingham

Illustrations by Bonna Rouse
Photographs by Marc Crabtree

Crabtree Publishing Company
www.crabtreebooks.com

Created by Bobbie Kalman

Dedicated by Marc Crabtree
For Trystan Jamie Jobin, because you're such an amazing person

Editor-in-Chief
Bobbie Kalman

Author
John Crossingham

Editorial director
Niki Walker

Project editor
Rebecca Sjonger

Editors
Amanda Bishop
Kathryn Smithyman

Art director
Robert MacGregor

Design
Margaret Amy Reiach
Campbell Creative Services (cover)

Production coordinator
Heather Fitzpatrick

Photo research
Rebecca Sjonger
Jaimie Nathan

Special thanks to
Jonathan King, Sunčana Selimović, Ivor Selimović,
Joan King, Ljiljana Selimović, Marc Crabtree

Consultant
Kalinda Mathis, Executive Director
International Inline Skating Association

Photographs
Marc Crabtree: pages 6, 10, 11, 12, 13, 14, 15, 16, 18, 19, 22,
    24, 25, 26, 27
Bruce Curtis: pages 4, 28
Other images by Corbis Images, Digital Stock, and PhotoDisc

Illustrations
All illustrations by Bonna Rouse except the following:
Trevor Morgan: page 6 (bottom)

Digital prepress
Embassy Graphics

Printer
Worzalla Publishing

Crabtree Publishing Company

www.crabtreebooks.com   1-800-387-7650

PMB 16A
350 Fifth Avenue
Suite 3308
New York, NY
10118

612 Welland Avenue
St. Catharines
Ontario
Canada
L2M 5V6

73 Lime Walk
Headington
Oxford
OX3 7AD
United Kingdom

Cataloging-in-Publication Data
Crossingham, John
 In-line skating in action / John Crossingham; illustrations by
Bonna Rouse; photographs by Marc Crabtree.
     p. cm. -- (Sports in action)
Includes index.
This book discusses basic movements and techniques of in-line
skating, recreational and competitive skating, safety tips, and more.
 ISBN 0-7787-0328-2 (RLB) -- ISBN 0-7787-0348-7 (pbk.)
 1. In-line skating--Juvenile literature. [1. In-line skating.]
I. Rouse, Bonna, ill. II. Crabtree, Marc, ill. III. Title. IV. Series.
 GV859.73 .C76 2003
 796.22--dc21

                                              LC 2002014296

Contents

What is in-line skating?

In-line skating is a great way to combine fun, transportation, and exercise. In-line skates are like ice skates, but they have a row of wheels instead of metal blades.

These wheels allow people to skate on pavement. People can usually use ice skates only in winter, but with in-line skates they can enjoy skating year-round.

Summertime blues

In-line skating began as an experiment. In the early 1980s, some professional ice hockey players wanted to practice in the summer, but it was too hot for ice to be made. Roller skates were already invented, but their wheels were side by side. They did not "feel" like ice skates. The hockey players wanted wheels that were in a line, like a skate's blade. The name "in-line" comes from the position of the skate's row of wheels.

All kinds of skating

Winter athletes, including figure skaters and hockey players, skate in the summer to keep their skills sharp. **Freestyle** in-line skating is a sport that's similar to figure skating. There are also competitive sports such as **in-line speed skating** and **roller hockey** that are similar to ice events, but they take place on pavement. Most people, however, use their skates as a fun way to exercise and get around.

On the edge

The most daring in-line sport is **aggressive skating**. Skaters leap off giant ramps and perform moves called **tricks** in midair. Sometimes they do tricks off everyday items such as benches, railings, and curbs. The tricks are often similar to those performed by skateboarders or BMX bicyclists.

In-line skating is a fun and healthy way for people of all ages to get around.

Aggressive skating is thrilling, but it is for experts only!

The essentials

Besides skates, safety gear is the most important equipment for in-line skating. You should never skate without a helmet and protective gear. A pair of shorts and a T-shirt are the best clothing to wear for in-line skating. You may want to wear a jacket, sweatshirt, or pants in cool weather.

Your helmet strap should be snug under your chin. If you can knock off your helmet by tapping the side of your head, the helmet is too loose.

Your pads can go over or under your clothes. Wear your pads on top of your clothing if you want to protect it as well as your body. Be sure the straps are snug but not too tight.

Your clothing should be comfortable and allow you to move easily. Use a light backpack if you need to carry extra items.

Your body can lose a lot of moisture as you skate. If you're going to be skating for a while, take a water bottle with you.

Buying your skates

When buying a pair of skates, try on several pairs to get the best fit. Your skates should be snug but not too tight. Skates are made for all age groups and genders, so be sure to ask the salesperson which is best for you. If you are renting skates, check them carefully for problems such as broken laces or worn-out brake pads.

tongue

binding

laces

toe

heel

frame

wheels

brake pad

Most in-line skates have four wheels, but some children's models have only three, and racing skates can have five.

Racing and aggressive models usually don't have brake pads. Not having brakes helps skaters perform specific tricks and skills.

Warming up

It's a good idea to stretch before heading out on your skates. Stretching warms up your muscles, which helps prevent painful sprains and strains that keep you on your couch instead of on your skates! Take five minutes to perform these simple stretches, and you're on your way.

Leg lunges
Stand with your feet wide apart. Bend your left knee until you feel a stretch on the inside of your right leg. Hold the stretch for a count of five. Straighten up and switch sides.

Ankle stretch
Sit on the ground with one leg straight. Bend your other leg so that you can grab your foot. Gently move it in circles. When you have done ten circles, do ten more in the other direction. Change legs.

Neck stretch
It's easy to hurt your neck, so do this stretch carefully. Tilt your head forward so that your chin points at your chest. Slowly roll your head toward one shoulder and then the other. Don't move your head farther than feels comfortable and never roll your head backward.

8

Quadriceps stretch

Stand on your right foot and use your right hand to support yourself against a wall or pole. Bring your left foot up behind you until you can grab it with your left hand. Pull gently until you feel the stretch in the front of your leg. Hold the stretch for a count of ten and then switch to your right leg.

Arm circles

Swing your arms in large circles. Make the motions smaller and smaller until your arms are moving in tiny circles straight out to the sides. Reverse the direction, starting with small circles and ending with giant circles.

9

Take it slow

Before you try to skate, you must learn how to balance. In-line skates are stiff, and even standing still in them feels strange at first. The best way to get comfortable is to walk while wearing the skates. Start by practicing on a surface that will keep you from rolling, such as carpet or grass.

Getting a stance

A **stance** is a body position you hold while skating. To find your **basic stance**, place your feet shoulder-width apart. Both feet should point straight ahead. Bend slightly at the knees and hips. Always keep your knees bent so that you can fall forward. Make sure your back is in a comfortable position and your bottom isn't sticking out.

In your basic stance, try a simple exercise such as bending at the knees. Get used to the feel of the skates and how you balance on them.

inside edges

Inside out

Each side of a skate's wheel is called an **edge**. Skaters use their edges to help them speed up, slow down, turn, and stop. Get familiar with your edges. Without moving your feet, move your knees toward each other. You'll naturally lean on the **inside edges** of the wheels. Now move your knees apart until you are leaning on the **outside edges**.

outside edges

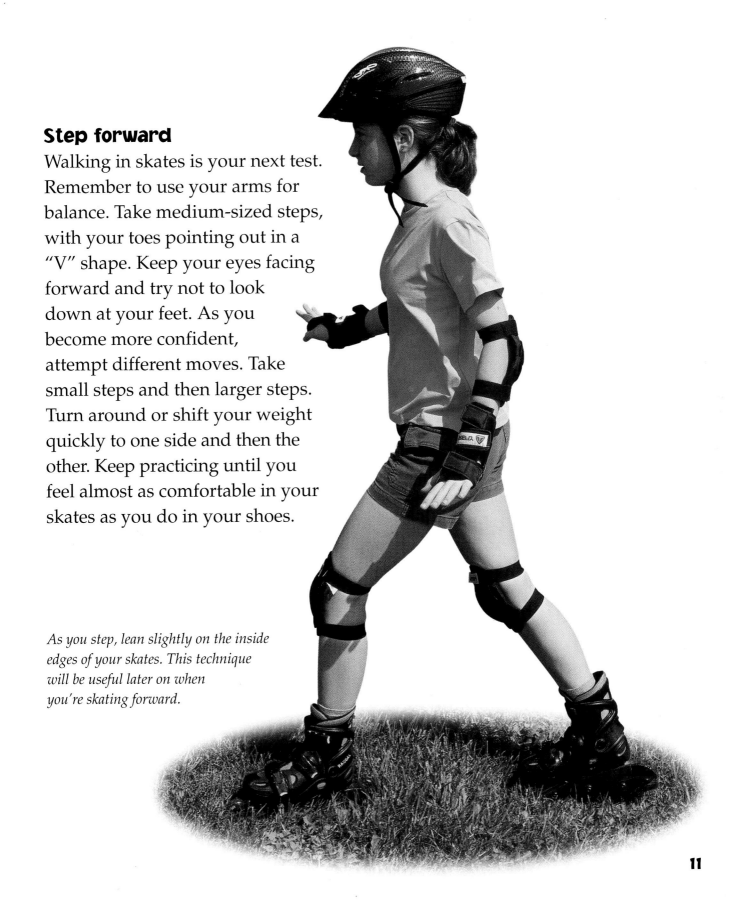

Step forward

Walking in skates is your next test. Remember to use your arms for balance. Take medium-sized steps, with your toes pointing out in a "V" shape. Keep your eyes facing forward and try not to look down at your feet. As you become more confident, attempt different moves. Take small steps and then larger steps. Turn around or shift your weight quickly to one side and then the other. Keep practicing until you feel almost as comfortable in your skates as you do in your shoes.

As you step, lean slightly on the inside edges of your skates. This technique will be useful later on when you're skating forward.

Come for a glide

There are two main movements in an in-line skating **stride—gliding** and **stroking**. Gliding happens when you roll across a surface. Stroking is the act of pushing against the ground. Balancing is difficult once your skates are rolling, so most beginners learn how to glide before they try stroking. Be sure to practice far away from traffic. Turn the page to read more about stroking.

Get rolling

Begin by getting into your basic stance. Hold on to a railing or a friend if you need help balancing. When you are ready to move, slowly lean forward and place your hands on your knees. Eventually, you'll start gliding. As you glide, you can keep your hands on your knees or try holding them out to the sides.

Test your balance

As you get comfortable gliding, you can test your balance. Try lifting one leg and gliding on the other. Switch legs. When gliding on a single leg, remember to center your body weight over that leg by bending your knee. For example, if you're gliding on your left leg, lean your upper body slightly to the left and bend your left knee. Learning to glide on one leg is important. You'll need to balance on a single leg in order to stroke.

Remember never to lean back when skating. If you lean too far back, your skates will fly out from under your body, and you'll fall on your bottom. Ouch!

Practice gliding on one leg at a time to test your balance.

How do I stop these things?

Good question! Once you get moving, you'll need to know how to stop. The easiest stop to learn is the **plow**. To stop, point your toes toward each other to form a "V." Lower your body slightly by bending at the knees and hips. Do not lean back. You'll slow down and come to a gentle stop.

Don't try to turn when you're learning to glide. Ask an adult to walk alongside you if you need help.

Handling a fall

Every skater falls at one time or another, so you should be prepared to take a tumble. There are different ways to fall, and some are better than others. Your best bet is always to fall forward. If you feel yourself losing balance, try to fall on your knees. You can use your knee, elbow, and wrist pads, as well as other protective gear, to help cushion the impact. To get up again, bring up one knee first and then try to stand.

Give it a push

Unless you are going downhill, gliding isn't a fast way to move. You need to stroke to build up speed. To stroke, you make a large backward push using one leg at a time. After you stroke with one leg, you glide on the other. Stroking isn't just leg movements, however. You use your whole body to gain speed and stay balanced. For example, as you stroke with your right leg, your upper body leans forward and over your left knee, which you bend for balance. This set of moves is called **lunging**. Lunging helps you keep your balance. The better you are at lunging, the harder you can push, and the faster you'll go.

1. Begin in your basic stance. Turn your right toe out. Dig your inside edge into the ground and push back. Lunge slightly over your left skate. You'll glide forward.

2. Lift your right skate and turn it forward. Bring it next to your left skate. Straighten up but keep your hips and knees slightly bent for balance.

3. Now stroke with your left leg and lunge to the right. Remember to dig in with your inside edge as you stroke. Glide on your right skate.

Taking it all in stride

Don't try to go too fast when you're learning to stroke. Enjoy performing one stroke at a time. Imagine this pattern: "Stroke right, glide, stroke left, glide," and so on. As you improve, you can try stroking and gliding nonstop. Performing strokes and glides one after the other is called **striding**. When striding, you begin a stroke with one skate just as the other returns to the glide position. Striding allows you to build up speed quickly. Keep your strides smooth and even. If your motions feel jerky, return to practicing the motions of your strokes.

Swizzle step

Swizzling is another way of moving forward. When you swizzle, your skates roll away from and then toward each other. They move along the ground in an hourglass pattern. Learning to swizzle will improve your control and help you get used to using your edges. Remember to hold out your arms in front of you for balance.

1. Stand in your basic stance. Point your toes away from each other and lean on your inside edges. Let both skates curve forward and outward.

2. Once your skates are far apart, turn the toes inward. Bring your skates back onto the centers of the wheels. Your skates should curve toward each other.

Stopping

As your skating improves, you'll outgrow the plow stop. You'll be ready to try some of the other ways of stopping. You can start by using your skate's built-in brake. The brake pad is usually found on the heel of the right skate (see page 7). If you prefer to use your left foot to brake, you can have the pad moved to your left skate. The brake pad allows you to stop more gracefully and with more control than the plow stop does. You use the brake pad by dragging it along the ground. To work well, this motion requires a proper stance.

Braking stance

The **braking stance** is very similar to your basic stance. To find your braking stance, build up some speed and glide along on two feet. Have your back straight and your knees bent. Move your braking foot slightly forward. Lift up the toe of your braking foot and push the pad against the ground with your heel. At the same time, bend your other leg and lower your bottom as though you are beginning to sit. Don't lean back! Leaning back will cause you to fall. Hold your arms out in front of you for balance.

Don't push down too hard with the brake pad. At first, your stops should be slow and gentle. As you become more confident, you can try quicker stops. Remember, the faster you stop, the lower your body should go.

Done to a "T"

The **drag stop**, or **T-stop**, is another useful braking style. The T-stop gets its name from the "T" you form with your skates as you brake. At first, practice the T-stop only when you're going slowly. When you're ready to stop, lift up your braking skate (the one with the brake pad). Turn the toe out to the side so that the inside of the skate faces forward. Place the braking skate about a foot (30 cm) behind your other skate to form a "T." Drag the wheels along the ground until you stop. Although the T-stop is useful, it wears out the inside edges of the wheels on your braking skate. The brake pad is still the best way to stop.

Keep your body weight centered over your front leg to prevent you from **spinning out**.

Carved turns

Now that you can glide, stroke, and brake, there's only one thing missing—turning! Being able to change direction is the final part of getting comfortable on your skates. Simple turns, called **carved turns**, are made using the skate's edges. To do one, you lean one skate on its outside edge and the other on its inside edge. You then just lean your body in the direction you wish to turn. Carved turns are also called **parallel turns** because your skates are parallel, or pointing in the same direction.

Carving it

The hardest part of learning carved turns is getting over the fear that you'll fall. Although you are leaning over to the side, and it feels like you could tip, the edges of your wheels are made to grip the pavement. As long as you have some speed, making carved turns is quite easy.

Try practicing your turns on a wide stretch of pavement with gentle curves and few obstacles.

A carved right turn

1. Begin by gliding on both skates. Lean to the right, leading with your shoulder. At the same time, slide your right foot forward and your left foot back.

2. Lean your right skate on its outside edge and your left skate on its inside edge. Try to keep your knees bent and your upper body over your right knee.

3. To end the turn, slide your right skate next to your left skate and bring both onto the centers of the wheels. Bring your upper body back to an upright position.

One step further

In a right turn, your right leg is your **leading leg**. Your left leg is the **trailing leg**. The opposite is true in a left turn. To improve your balance, try leaning only on the leading leg during a turn. Lift up your trailing leg and use your arms for balance.

The faster you are moving, the more you have to bend into the turn. To handle higher speeds, spread your feet apart slightly more than usual. As you lean, keep your upper body over your leading leg. When you want to end the turn, shift your weight onto your other leg.

Crossover turns

During carved turns, you lose speed as you turn. **Crossover turns** allow you to build up speed while turning. These turns are named after the way your feet cross over each other to make the turn. Crossover turns, or **crossovers**, are common in ice skating. To perform them, you must be comfortable balancing on one foot as you turn. Practice that motion often before you try crossovers.

In step

Before trying a turn while skating, practice crossing your feet over each other while standing. Bring one foot across in front of the other and set it down so that your legs are crossed. Lift your back foot and move it next to the front one so that they are side by side again. You can practice this motion on grass or carpeting, with or without your skates on. Later, you can try crossovers as you glide.

Fancy feet

Crossover turns are difficult to learn, so don't be discouraged if you don't master them right away. Remember that during a crossover, your upper body leans into the turn, much as it does in a carved turn. Practice doing a right crossover as described below and then switch the instructions to practice left crossover turns.

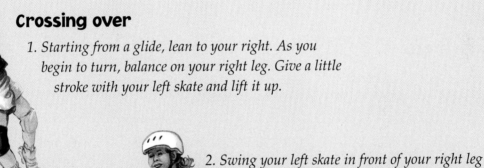

Crossing over

1. *Starting from a glide, lean to your right. As you begin to turn, balance on your right leg. Give a little stroke with your left skate and lift it up.*

2. *Swing your left skate in front of your right leg and place it down on the other side. Place the **ball**, or front half, of your left skate down first. Give a little stroke with your right skate and lift it up. Now balance and glide on your left skate.*

3. *Swing your right skate behind your left leg. Place your right skate down, ball first, next to your left skate. Straighten your upper body and begin to stroke straight ahead out of the turn.*

Note: The larger the crossover turn, the more times your skates will cross each other before the turn ends. As you improve, you'll be able to judge how many times you need to cross over by the speed you are going and the size of the turn.

Skating backward

You don't really need to know how to skate backward, but mastering this skill is great for your confidence. It's also a lot of fun! Skating backward is easier than it looks. It involves making gentle wave patterns with your skates. It's best to start with the **backward swizzle** and the **wiggle**. For both moves, your skates stay on the ground.

(left) When skating backward, it's helpful to imagine that you are leading with your lower body. Always look over your shoulder so you can see where you're going!

Backward swizzle

The backward swizzle is similar to the forward swizzle (page 15). You create the same hourglass patterns with your skates, but in reverse. These pictures show you how it's done.

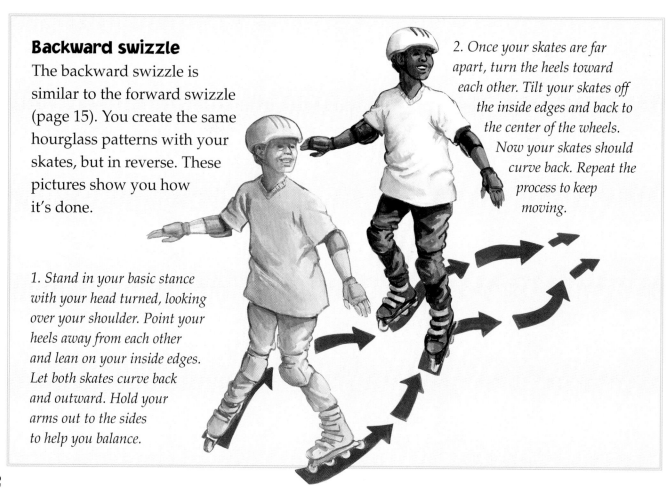

2. Once your skates are far apart, turn the heels toward each other. Tilt your skates off the inside edges and back to the center of the wheels. Now your skates should curve back. Repeat the process to keep moving.

1. Stand in your basic stance with your head turned, looking over your shoulder. Point your heels away from each other and lean on your inside edges. Let both skates curve back and outward. Hold your arms out to the sides to help you balance.

The wiggle

The motions in the wiggle, shown below, are similar to those of the swizzle. You look over your shoulder, and your skates curve in and out. Instead of moving your legs at the same time, however, you move them one at a time. It's easier to balance with your hands out in front of you rather than to the sides. The wiggle is also known as **backward stroking**.

Getting tricky

It's possible to do more complex moves, such as crossovers, while skating backward. These motions are very difficult, however. A lot of skaters never learn them! When you want to turn while skating backward, use your edges to perform carved turns. If you want to learn more difficult moves, find a skilled instructor who can teach you.

1. Begin in the basic stance and look over your shoulder. Lean on the inside edge of your left skate and push out your heel. Keep your right skate straight.

3. When your skates are parallel again, lean on the inside edge of your right skate. Let it curve away and then pull it back toward your body.

2. Come off the inside edge of your left skate and curve your heel back toward your body.

Over the hills

No matter where you skate, you are bound to be on a hill at some point. Skating on hills can be exciting, but you must be very careful. In fact, you should only try skating down a hill if you are confident that you can stop safely. If you have any doubts, you should just take off your skates and walk down the hill. These pages have some tips for going up and down hills when you feel ready.

Going up

Bicycles have gears that cyclists shift to make riding up hills easier. In-line skaters, however, rely only on muscle power to move up a hill. Skating uphill really tests your striding ability. It requires more effort than skating on flat ground. You must dig in hard with your inside edges and use your upper body to lunge with each stroke. These motions create more **momentum**, or forward power, in your skating. Finally, skate with your weight on the balls of your feet, not on your heels, just as you would while running up a set of stairs.

As you approach a hill, build up as much speed as you can. You'll need it!

Down we go!

Skating uphill is tiring, but skating downhill can be dangerous! High-speed crashes can cause serious injuries. If you want to tackle a hill, start on a small one with a gentle slope.

On guard

You should always be ready to brake when going downhill. Keep your braking foot slightly in front of you so that you can just lift your toe and tap your brake pad against the ground when you need to slow down. Keep your back straight and your knees bent. Bent knees help **absorb**, or cushion, any bumps you hit. Have your arms steady and bent at the elbows. If you feel yourself losing control, crouch down and brake evenly—don't panic!

When going downhill, make sure you look ahead at all times. If you see an obstacle coming up, slow down and then move around it.

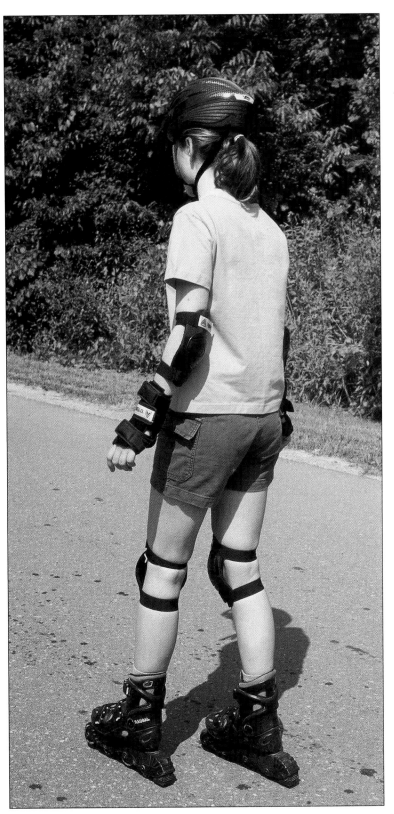

Street smarts

Skating around a city is much different than skating through a park. Cars, curbs, cyclists, sewer drains, and uneven sidewalks are just a few of the hazards you'll face. Safety gear is always needed, but it is especially important that you

CAUTION
CRACK SEALING IN PAVEMENT MAY CAUSE A TRIP HAZARD TO IN-LINE SKATERS
PROCEED WITH CAUTION

wear it on the street. If you want to skate through the city, you must be able to stop and turn quickly without problems. If you doubt your ability to perform any of the basic skating skills described in this book, stay away from traffic!

Hitting the grass

One of the most common obstacles is grass. Nothing slows you more quickly than hitting a patch of grass—it's like skating onto glue! If you're heading for grass or sand and can't avoid it, put one foot in front of the other in a line. Stick your arms out in front of you. As you slow down, bring your feet back side by side.

Just grate

Streets are full of hazards like potholes and sewer grates. You can skate safely over grates—just make sure that your skates aren't in line with the vents, or your wheels will get stuck and you'll fall forward. Keep one foot ahead of the other and both skates pointed in the same direction.

On the road

Skaters move on the street with the flow of traffic. In North America, cars and skaters use the right-hand side of the road. As an in-line skater, you follow street rules

similar to those of cyclists, which means you must obey all road signs and traffic lights. Always use your brake pad to stop in traffic. Doing so gives you the most control and allows you to stop in a straight line.

After dark

If you're skating in the evening, wear bright or reflective clothing so that motorists and cyclists can see you. You can also put reflective stickers on the back and sides of your helmet.

Find your space

Plan your route before you head into the city on your skates. Look at a map with an adult and decide the safest course to travel. Many cities and towns have paths that are for skaters, runners, and cyclists only. Use these paths as much as you can. The route with the least traffic is always your best bet.

Curbs are quite easy to handle. If you want to get up onto a curb, simply skate alongside it. Lift up the leg closest to the curb and glide on the other leg. Step onto the curb with the nearest leg and then move your other leg up on the curb.

You may not be in a car, but you aren't a pedestrian when you skate. Always make way for people who are walking.

Roller hockey

Roller hockey, or **in-line hockey**, is a sport that is similar to ice hockey. There are two teams, and each one tries to score goals by shooting the **puck** or ball into the other team's net. The team with the most goals at the end of the game wins. Players use many of the same helmets, pads, sticks, and gloves that ice hockey players use.

What's the difference?

Like ice hockey, roller hockey is played on a surface called a **rink**, shown below right, but the rink's surface is smooth pavement rather than ice. Instead of three **periods**, many roller hockey games have only two periods. Depending on the age group of the players, the periods can last from ten to 25 minutes.

Who's on my team?

A roller hockey team usually has five players instead of ice hockey's six players. The **goalie** protects the net. Two **forwards** try to score on their opponent's net. Two **defense** players assist the goalie and get the ball or puck to the forwards. Some teams have an extra forward called a **center**.

Helping you improve

If you want to play roller hockey well, you have to be a great skater. You need to have strong turning, stopping, and striding skills. Playing roller hockey can help average skaters improve, however. Even if you aren't a great skater yet, there are many levels of competition. Playing in a beginner's league can be a lot of fun, and it's also an excellent way to learn better skating techniques from a coach.

Playing pick-up

If there's no roller hockey league where you live, try playing with friends. A few hockey sticks, a ball, a net, and your regular safety gear are all you need. Just remember to keep the game clean—**checking**, or hitting with your body or stick, isn't allowed!

Roller pucks

In ice hockey, the puck is a hard rubber disc. Roller hockey pucks are also discs, but they have small ball bearings that allow them to glide across the rink. Some roller hockey players use a hard rubber ball instead of a puck. The ball is about the same size as a tennis ball.

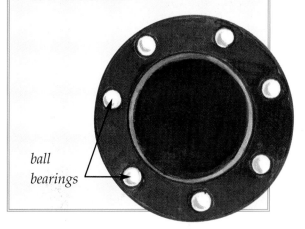

ball bearings

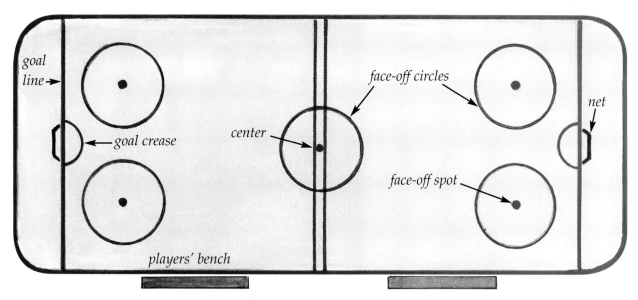

goal line

goal crease

center

face-off circles

net

face-off spot

players' bench

Aggressive skating

The most thrilling in-line skating sport is aggressive skating. This challenging sport is for experts only! Aggressive tricks combine balance with smooth, spinning leaps over obstacles. These objects can be anything a skater chooses—the most common are railings, benches, and ramps. Aggressive skaters who ride giant ramps perform **vertical skating**.

Pipe dreams
Giant ramps are called **pipe ramps** because they are curved like the inside of a pipe. The most common pipe ramps are **quarter-pipes**, which have one slope, and **half-pipes**, which have two joined slopes that face each other.

*Pipe ramps allow skaters to get a lot of **air**, or space between themselves and the obstacle.*

Up in the air

Midair tricks, or **aerials**, are some of the most exciting in the sport. For an aerial, the skater first builds up speed on the ramp. He or she then flies off the **coping**, or top edge of the ramp. Once in the air, the skater can perform one of dozens of tricks.

Move your body

Skaters also perform tricks by moving into body positions in midair. They tuck in their legs, grab a skate with one hand, or kick out a leg. Each body position has a different trick name. For instance, a skater balances on a ramp's coping with one hand to perform a **handplant**. In aggressive competitions, skaters are judged on both the difficulty of their tricks and how well they perform them.

Back to the grind

Many tricks involve skaters sliding along railings and bars. Instead of rolling on them, though, skaters **grind** them. Grinding happens when skaters slide along objects with the sides of their wheels. Some models of aggressive skates have smaller middle wheels to make grinding easier. Even with these skates, grinding requires excellent balance. Skaters change their foot positions to make the grinds more challenging.

So you want to try this stuff? Be sure to practice tricks with an instructor who can teach you proper techniques. Aggressive skating is fun, but it's also hard work.

Glossary

Note: Boldfaced words that are defined in the book may not appear in the glossary.

aerial A trick performed in midair

aggressive skating In-line skating that involves daring jumps and tricks

basic stance The body position a skater usually holds while he or she is skating

crossover A fast turn that requires one foot to cross over the other

freestyle skating A style of skating made up of moves and tricks chosen by the skater

glide To roll across a surface

handplant A stunt done by a skater who puts one hand on the ground and both feet in the air

period A set amount of time played in a hockey game before a break

roller hockey The game of hockey that is played on a cement surface by players in in-line skates

spinning out The act of going into a spin on in-line skates which can send an inexperienced skater out of control

stride A single "step" made up of a stroke and a glide

stroke To push off with one skate in order to glide on the other

swizzle To roll forward or backward by alternately leaning on the inside and outside edges of the wheels

vertical skating Skating on ramps that launch the skater into the air

Index

1 2 3 4 5 6 7 8 9 0   Printed in the U.S.A. 2 1 0 9 8 7 6 5 4 3